Conquer Your Fears in 7 Steps

Conquer Your Fears in 7 Steps

A Comprehensive Guide

B. Vincent

QuillQuest Publishers

Contents

Introduction **1**

1 Chapter 1: Understanding Your Fear **4**

2 Chapter 2: Step 1 – Acknowledgment **8**

3 Chapter 3: Step 2 – Self-Reflection **12**

4 Chapter 4: Step 3 – Education **16**

5 Chapter 5: Step 4 – Preparation **19**

6 Chapter 6: Step 5 – Exposure **22**

7 Chapter 7: Step 6 – Acceptance and Adjustment **25**

8 Chapter 8: Step 7 – Mastery **28**

Conclusion **31**

Appendices **33**

Introduction

Introductory statements

In the excursion of life, dread stands as both a watchman and a guardian. It fills in as a gatekeeper by making us aware of genuine risks, guaranteeing our endurance and security. However, it likewise goes about as a watchman, frequently remaining among us and our fullest potential, our most profound longings, and our most genuine selves. Across ages and civilizations, dread has been a vital power molding choices, activities, and eventually, predeterminations.

The Significance of Vanquishing Fears

The mission to overcome dread isn't simply about eliminating a deterrent; it's tied in with opening a way to another range of potential outcomes. Envision carrying on with a day to day existence where dread no longer directs your decisions, where every choice is made not out of evasion, but rather out of trust, desire, and a significant feeling of direction. This isn't a dream. It's a truly feasible reality. Vanquishing dread doesn't mean living unafraid; it implies figuring out how to live past the imperatives it forces, grasping its mechanics, and excelling at exploring through it.

In this extensive aide, we set out on an extraordinary excursion — a bit by bit journey through the layers of dread and the most common way of recovering the power it has held over us. This book is planned as a read as well as an encounter, a progression of disclosures that will challenge you, support you, and eventually engage you to make dread your partner instead of your foe.

Outline of the 7 Stages

The way to vanquishing your feelings of dread is organized around seven vital stages, each filling in as an achievement in this excursion of change. These means are not convenient solutions yet significant cycles that address dread at its foundations, cultivating a profound, enduring change.

1. Acknowledgment: The initial step is tied in with recognizing the truth about dread. It's tied in with uncovering it, perceiving its presence, and grasping its tendency. This step is critical for it lays the basis for all that follows.

2. Self-Reflection: Here, we turn the focal point internal, inspecting the stories and convictions that fuel our apprehensions. Self-reflection makes the way for mindfulness, a vital fixing during the time spent beating fears.

3. Education: Information is power. Grasping the beginnings, brain science, and systems of dread demystifies it, lessening its hold over us. This step includes gaining both from research and from the insight of the individuals who have strolled this way before us.

4. Preparation: Vanquishing dread requires both mental and commonsense status. This step centers around furnishing ourselves with the devices, techniques, and attitude expected to straightforwardly overcome our apprehensions.

5. Exposure: Progressive, controlled openness to the wellspring of our feelings of trepidation is a demonstrated strategy for conquering them. This step is turning around what we dread in a strong, sensible way, building flexibility as we go.

6. Acceptance and Change: This step includes tolerating dread as a piece of the human experience, figuring out how to coincide with it, and changing our reactions to it. It's about adaptability, strength, and the insight to observe what we

have some control over and what we should figure out how to live with.

7. Mastery: The last step is tied in with coordinating what we've realized into our lives, transforming our excursion into an economical act of dread administration and self-improvement. Authority isn't tied in with annihilating apprehension yet about turning into the expert of our own insight, picking how we answer dread, and in this manner, how we explore our lives.

This book, "Overcome Your Feelings of dread in 7 Stages: An Extensive Aide," is something other than a manual; it's a friend in your excursion towards a more brave life. It's loaded with experiences, viable exhortation, activities, and genuine stories that will direct, rouse, and support you constantly.

The Excursion Ahead

As you turn these pages, you're not simply perusing a book; you're venturing out on a significant excursion of change. This excursion is about something beyond conquering dread; it's tied in with rediscovering your power, your true capacity, and your capacity to mold your life's course. With each step, you'll uncover a greater amount of your internal strength, look into your actual self, and open degrees of opportunity and satisfaction that dread has kept under control.

Get ready to set out on one of the main undertakings of your life — an experience that starts with a solitary step in the right direction, a stage away from dread and towards the boundless potential that looks for you past it.

Chapter 1: Understanding Your Fear

The Idea of Dread

Dread, in its most base structure, is an endurance system. An intrinsic reaction shields us from risk, a basic part of the human condition that has developed over centuries. However, in the cutting edge world, where actual dangers are less continuous, dread frequently appears in light of mental and prevailing burdens, turning into a more unavoidable and less unmistakable power in our lives.

To comprehend dread is to perceive its duality: it is both a defender and a persecutor. It can save us from hurt, yet it can likewise keep us from seeking after amazing open doors and encounters that could enhance our lives. This duality is at the core of dread's intricacy, making it a difficult enemy yet additionally an expected partner.

Distinguishing Your Feelings of dread

The most vital move toward understanding your trepidation is to recognize it. Fears can be expansive and conceptual, similar to the apprehension about disappointment or dismissal, or they can be explicit and situational, like the apprehension about levels or public talking. Distinguishing your apprehensions requires genuineness and weakness, as it includes going up against parts of yourself and your life that you might have stayed away from or stifled.

Begin by asking yourself:

•What circumstances cause me to feel restless or apprehensive?

•Are there explicit triggers that get a trepidation reaction?

•How would I respond genuinely and sincerely when I'm apprehensive?

Recording your feelings of trepidation in a diary can be a useful asset for acknowledgment and reflection. It permits you to see designs, figure out triggers, and start the most common way of tending to your apprehensions with clearness and expectation.

The Brain research Behind Dread

Dread works on both an organic and mental level. Naturally, dread triggers the "survival" reaction, a progression of physiological changes that set up the body to defy or get away from an apparent danger. Mentally, dread is affected by private encounters, social standards, and learned ways of behaving.

Understanding the brain science behind your feelings of dread includes investigating their starting points. Many apprehensions come from previous encounters, injuries, or gained ways of behaving from compelling figures in our lives. By analyzing the foundations of our feelings of dread, we can start to comprehend their hold over us and begin the most common way of unraveling from their grasp.

Mental Mutilations and Dread

Mental bends, or nonsensical idea designs, assume a huge part by they way we see and respond to fear. Normal bends incorporate catastrophizing (anticipating the absolute worst result), overgeneralization (accepting that a pessimistic occasion will happen more than once), and personalization (accepting that occasions are straightforwardly connected with oneself, in any event, when they are not).

Perceiving and testing these bends is a basic move toward understanding and overseeing dread. Mental social treatment (CBT) methods, for example, journaling and mental rebuilding, can be successful instruments for distinguishing and changing twisted thought designs.

Overcoming Your Feelings of trepidation

Standing up to your feelings of trepidation isn't tied in with disposing of them completely yet about figuring out how to live with them such that they never again control your activities and choices. This interaction starts with understanding, which then, at that point, prompts affirmation and, at last, to activity.

Pragmatic strides for overcoming your feelings of trepidation include:

•Openness: Steadily presenting yourself to the wellspring of your trepidation in a controlled and safe way can assist with lessening the apprehension reaction over the long haul.

•Unwinding Procedures: Practices like profound breathing, reflection, and care can assist with dealing with the physical and close to home side effects of dread.

•Looking for Help: Conversing with companions, family, or an expert can furnish you with viewpoint, support, and methodologies for adapting to your feelings of trepidation.

The Force of Versatility

Building versatility is a fundamental piece of understanding and overseeing dread. Flexibility isn't tied in with being courageous however about returning quickly from unfortunate encounters with strength and elegance. It includes fostering an outlook that perspectives challenges as any open doors for development and learning, instead of as inconceivable obstructions.

Methodologies for building versatility include:

•Keeping an Uplifting perspective: Zeroing in on the positive parts of a circumstance, even notwithstanding dread, can assist with cultivating versatility.

•Building an Encouraging group of people: Having areas of strength for a framework can give a conviction that all is good and having a place, which is critical in the midst of dread and vulnerability.

•Embracing Change: Review change as an unavoidable and reasonable piece of life can assist with diminishing apprehension and tension connected with the unexplored world.

Understanding your apprehension is the most important move toward vanquishing it. By perceiving the idea of dread, recognizing your own feelings of trepidation, figuring out the brain science behind them, and finding a way reasonable ways to confront them, you start the excursion toward a more brave and satisfying life. This section has established the groundwork for that excursion, giving you the instruments and information to recognize your feelings of dread and begin the method involved with beating them.

As we push ahead to the following section, we will dive further into the initial step of overcoming your apprehensions: Affirmation. This significant stage is where the excursion of change genuinely starts, making way for the significant work that lies ahead.

Chapter 2: Step 1 – Acknowledgment

The Significance of Recognizing Dread

Affirmation is the cognizant acknowledgment of dread's presence in our lives. It's turning around the reality of our feelings, without refusal or evasion. This step is pivotal in light of the fact that it shifts dread from an unclear shadow that weavers our subliminal to an unmistakable test that we can address and survive.

Large numbers of us burn through significant effort denying our feelings of dread, covering them under layers of justification, or veiling them with different feelings. Notwithstanding, unacknowledged trepidation has an approach to developing, influencing our choices, ways of behaving, and at last, the nature of our lives. By recognizing our apprehensions, we venture out in recovering command over our feelings and our life's bearing.

Breaking the Pattern of Forswearing

The pattern of forswearing is a typical reaction to fear. A guard system shields us from prompt profound distress however, over the long haul, frustrates our development and prosperity. Breaking this cycle requires fortitude and self-empathy. It includes a readiness to confront awkward bits of insight and the comprehension that affirmation is definitely not an indication of shortcoming yet of solidarity.

One compelling method for breaking the pattern of refusal is through intelligent composition. By journaling about our feelings of dread, we give them a name and a shape, making them not so much scary but rather more sensible. This exercise works with affirmation as well as improves mindfulness, giving bits of knowledge into the idea of our apprehensions and how they impact our lives.

Techniques for Powerful Affirmation

Recognizing dread is something other than conceding its presence; it's tied in with grasping its unique situation, its triggers, and its effect. The following are a few systems to make this interaction more successful:

1. Name Your Trepidation: Distinguish and name your feelings of dread as explicitly as could really be expected. Naming your apprehension diminishes its vagueness and power.
2. Accept Your Weakness: Perceive that weakness is a piece of being human. Tolerating your weakness despite dread is a stage towards strengthening.
3. Understand the Triggers: Distinguish the circumstances, considerations, or sentiments that trigger your trepidation. Understanding these triggers can help you expect and deal with your apprehension reaction.
4. Reflect on Past Experiences: Consider how you've managed comparable apprehensions previously. Thinking about past experiences with dread can give significant bits of knowledge and methodologies to dealing with your ongoing apprehensions.

5. Share Your Feelings of dread: Discussing your apprehensions with confided in companions, family, or a specialist can offer help, point of view, and approval. Sharing your apprehensions diminishes their close to home hold and can enlighten pathways through them.

Practices for Recognizing Your Apprehensions

To work with the course of affirmation, here are pragmatic activities intended to go up against and articulate your apprehensions:

•Dread Planning: Make a visual guide of your feelings of trepidation, including their sources, triggers, and how they interconnect. This exercise can assist you with grasping the scene of your feelings of trepidation and distinguish regions for centered consideration.

•Letter to Your Trepidation: Compose a letter to your apprehension, tending to it straightforwardly. This exercise empowers a discourse with your trepidation, assisting you with communicating your sentiments and expectations towards it.

•The Worst situation imaginable Activity: Consider the worst situation imaginable related with your trepidation, then fundamentally assess the probability and ramifications of this situation. This exercise assists with placing fears into viewpoint, frequently uncovering that the results we dread are either improbable or sensible.

•Appreciation Reflection: For each dread recognized, list parts of the circumstance or your life for which you are thankful. This exercise assists shift with centering from dread to appreciation, adjusting your close to home point of view.

The Force of Affirmation in real life

Recognizing your feelings of trepidation is the most important move towards strengthening. It changes dread from a mind-boggling force into a test that can be perceived, made due, and survive. This step isn't tied in with disposing of dread yet about building another relationship with it — one where dread illuminates however doesn't control your choices and activities.

Through affirmation, we likewise develop strength, compassion, and mental fortitude. We discover that overcoming our feelings of trepidation, however awkward, is a significant demonstration of taking care of oneself and development. This acknowledgment is enabling, making way for the extraordinary work that follows.

Affirmation is the fundamental initial phase in overcoming your apprehensions. It is the establishment whereupon the excursion of defeating dread is assembled. By recognizing your feelings of dread, you start to demystify them, diminishing their power and opening up additional opportunities for development and satisfaction.

As we push ahead in this excursion, the subsequent stage will expand on the groundwork of affirmation, directing you towards more profound self-reflection and understanding. The way forward is one of disclosure, challenge, and change, and everything starts with the straightforward yet significant demonstration of recognizing your apprehensions.

{ **3** }

Chapter 3: Step 2 – Self-Reflection

The Job of Self-Appearance in Conquering Dread

Self-reflection is the purposeful demonstration of analyzing one's contemplations, sentiments, and inspirations. It is a vital stage in the excursion to overcome fears, as it permits us to uncover the fundamental convictions and encounters that fuel our feelings of trepidation. By understanding the underlying foundations of our feelings of dread, we can start to challenge and change the stories that keep us down, working with a course of real change.

Grasping the Starting points of Your Apprehensions

Fears frequently have well established starting points that can be followed back to previous encounters, injuries, cultural messages, or gained ways of behaving from family and other compelling figures. These beginnings shape our conviction frameworks and impact how we view ourselves and our general surroundings. Recognizing the wellspring of our apprehensions is fundamental for figuring out their effect and creating methodologies to defeat them.

Procedures for Compelling Self-Reflection

Participating in self-reflection requires persistence, trustworthiness, and a non-critical demeanor towards oneself. The following are a few procedures to direct you through this contemplative interaction:

1. Journaling: Expounding on your viewpoints, sentiments, and encounters can assist with explaining your feelings of trepidation and the conditions that trigger them. Diary prompts zeroed in on dread can be especially adroit.
2. Meditation and Care: These practices can assist with stilling the psyche, making it simpler to notice your considerations and feelings without connection. This increased mindfulness is priceless for self-reflection.
3. Therapy or Directing: Proficient direction can offer new points of view, assisting you with investigating the profundities of your feelings of trepidation in a protected and strong climate.
4. Questioning and Testing Convictions: Effectively scrutinizing the legitimacy and starting points of your convictions about dread can uncover bits of knowledge into how these convictions were framed and the way that they impact your way of behaving.

Practices for Developing Self-Reflection

To work with a more profound commitment with self-reflection, the accompanying activities can be especially powerful:

•The Five Whys Exercise: When you distinguish a trepidation, ask yourself "Why?" multiple times, each time going further into the clarification of your trepidation. This method can assist with uncovering the main driver of your trepidation.

•Life Timetable: Make a course of events of your life, featuring minutes that have essentially influenced your view of dread. This visual portrayal can assist you with interfacing previous encounters with current apprehensions.

•Conviction Challenge Worksheet: Rundown your convictions about your apprehensions and afterward challenge them by giving proof against these convictions. This exercise supports a basic assessment of the stories you hold about your feelings of dread.

The Extraordinary Force of Self-Reflection

Self-reflection not just guides in grasping the starting points and nature of our apprehensions yet additionally enables us to assume command of them. It works with a shift from being receptive to being proactive in managing dread, empowering us to settle on decisions in view of knowledge and seeing as opposed to programmed reactions.

Through self-reflection, we can likewise develop self-sympathy, perceiving that our feelings of dread don't characterize us. We figure out how to treat ourselves with benevolence and understanding, recognizing our feelings of trepidation while additionally perceiving our solidarity and strength in confronting them.

Exploring the Difficulties of Self-Reflection

Self-reflection can challenge, as it frequently includes going up against awkward bits of insight about ourselves and our past. It's vital to move toward this cycle with persistence and to focus on taking care of oneself. If self-reflection becomes overpowering, looking for help from companions, family, or emotional well-being experts can give the vital solace and direction.

Self-reflection is a basic move toward the excursion to vanquish your feelings of trepidation. It gives the experiences expected to comprehend the underlying foundations of your apprehensions, challenge restricting convictions, and at last, change your relationship with dread. This profound reflection makes ready for the subsequent stages in your excursion, where you'll figure out how to teach yourself about dread, plan intellectually and genuinely to confront it, and slowly open yourself to the wellsprings of your trepidation in a controlled and reasonable manner.

As we keep on investigating the moves toward vanquish dread, recall that self-reflection is a continuous cycle. It's a device for beating dread as well as for self-awareness and self-disclosure. The experiences acquired through self-reflection will act as a directing light as we push ahead to the following section, zeroing in on schooling as a way to demystify and lessen the force of dread.

{ 4 }

Chapter 4: Step 3 – Education

Grasping the Job of Training in Overcoming Dread

Schooling around one's feelings of dread is critical in changing questions into sensible difficulties. This part investigates how acquiring information about our feelings of dread can demystify them, decrease their profound grasp, and engage us with procedures to confront and defeat them.

The Force of Information

•The part opens with a conversation on how figuring out the mechanics, beginnings, and normal responses to dread can fundamentally diminish its effect.

•Featuring accounts of people who have conquered their feelings of trepidation through instruction, delineating the groundbreaking force of information.

Demystifying Dread

•An inside and out take a gander at the organic, mental, and social parts of dread.

•Master bits of knowledge into how fears create, and how deception or absence of understanding can intensify fears.

Procedures for Instructing Yourself About Your Feelings of trepidation

1. Research: Empowering perusers to explore their particular apprehensions, grasping normal triggers, and reactions. This segment remembers direction for tracking down solid well-springs of data.
2. Professional Direction: The significance of looking for data from experts, for example, advisors or specialists in the field connected with one's trepidation.
3. Learning from Others: Utilizing books, narratives, and on-line gatherings where people share their encounters of conquering comparable feelings of dread. This part underlines the instructive worth of shared encounters.

Functional Uses of Dread Training

•Fostering a Trepidation The executives Plan: Utilizing the information acquired to make a customized plan to confront and oversee fears.

•Risk Appraisal and The executives: Training perusers to survey the genuine dangers implied in their dreaded situations versus saw chances, utilizing schooling to overcome any issues between silly apprehensions and reality.

•Mental Social Methods: Prologue to mental conduct procedures that can help reexamine and decrease fears, underlining the job of training in these strategies.

Practices for Upgrading Dread Training

•Data Social event Exercise: A bit by bit manual for investigating a particular trepidation, recognizing dependable sources, and summing up key discoveries.

•Interview Task: Empowering perusers to talk with somebody who has effectively defeated a comparable trepidation, zeroing in on the instructive experiences from these individual stories.

•Fantasy versus Truth: A movement intended to distinguish and expose normal fantasies connected with their feelings of dread, building up the significance of exact data.

Beating Difficulties in Dread Schooling

•Managing Data Over-burden: Techniques to oversee overpowering measures of data without intensifying feelings of trepidation.

•Knowing Dependable Sources: Ways to distinguish reliable and deductively upheld data in the midst of falsehood.

The Excursion Proceeds: From Training to Arrangement

•The part closes by connecting the schooling about fears to the subsequent stage in the excursion: Readiness. It makes way for perusers to utilize their freshly discovered information to get ready intellectually and truly to go up against and defeat their feelings of trepidation.

•A mystery prologue to the following section, underscoring that schooling isn't just about realizing what dread is yet additionally about setting oneself up to make proactive strides against it.

{ 5 }

Chapter 5: Step 4 – Preparation

The Substance of Arrangement

The part opens by featuring the basic job that arrangement plays in the excursion to overcome fears. It frames how readiness overcomes any barrier between figuring out one's feelings of trepidation and effectively beating them. This segment underscores that exhaustive readiness is both a psychological and an actual cycle that fundamentally expands the opportunities to effectively overcome and vanquishing fears.

Mental Readiness: Building a Strong Outlook

•Developing an Uplifting perspective: Strategies for fostering a mentality that spotlights on sure results and versatility despite challenges.

•Representation Strategies: Directing perusers through the method involved with envisioning achievement, which can assist with diminishing uneasiness and construct certainty.

•Setting Reasonable Assumptions: Conversation on the significance of defining attainable objectives and assumptions to stay away from frustration and keep up with inspiration.

Actual Planning: Preparing the Body

•Stress Decrease Procedures: Presenting actual activities and unwinding methods that can assist with bringing down the body's pressure reaction while overcoming fears.

•Solid Way of life Decisions: Investigating how sustenance, exercise, and rest can support physical and emotional wellness, making it simpler to handle fears.

The Job of Arranging in Planning

•Fostering a Trepidation Conflict Plan: Bit by bit direction on making a point by point intend to confront fears, including gradual objectives and methodologies to oversee expected mishaps.

•Planning Through Recreation: Empowering perusers to mimic or practice overcoming their feelings of trepidation in a controlled climate, if conceivable, to acquire commonality and decrease uneasiness.

Apparatuses and Procedures for Powerful Arrangement

•Mental Rebuilding: Showing perusers how to challenge and change negative idea designs that can thwart their planning endeavors.

•Care and Contemplation: Itemized rehearses for keeping up with present-second mindfulness, which can reduce dread instigated pressure.

•Breathing Activities: Straightforward yet powerful breathing procedures to control physiological reactions to fear.

Practices for Improving Planning

•Objective Setting Worksheet: An organized activity to assist perusers with setting explicit, quantifiable, reachable, significant, and time-bound (Shrewd) objectives for overcoming their feelings of dread.

•Unwinding Practice Timetable: A manual for integrating unwinding rehearses into everyday schedules, holding back nothing in overseeing dread reactions.

•Perception Diary: Directions for keeping a diary devoted to picturing achievement, including prompts to envision conquering dread and accomplishing objectives.

Exploring the Difficulties of Planning

•Beating Overpreparation: Addressing the inclination to overprepare as a type of stalling, and how to perceive when now is the right time to make a move.

•Managing Pre-Activity Uneasiness: Procedures for overseeing nervousness that emerges during the arrangement stage, guaranteeing it doesn't upset progress towards facing fears.

Progressing from Arrangement to Activity

The section finishes up by stressing that readiness, while fundamental, is at last a forerunner to activity. It makes way for the following period of the excursion, which includes straightforwardly going up against fears through slow openness. This segment inspires perusers to change from wanting to doing, guaranteeing them that they are exceptional to overcome their apprehensions with certainty and versatility.

•Readiness Agenda: Giving a last agenda to guarantee perusers are completely ready, intellectually and truly, to make the following stride.

•Consolation for the Excursion Ahead: A persuasive shutting that reaffirms the peruser's capacity to beat their feelings of dread, empowering them to embrace the development and strengthening that looks for them in the resulting steps.

Chapter 6: Step 5 - Exposure

Prologue to Openness

The section starts by characterizing openness as a purposeful, controlled course of confronting fears, making sense of its establishing in mental exploration as a profoundly successful technique for dread decrease. This segment stresses the significance of expanding on the readiness work from the past section, guaranteeing perusers comprehend that openness is both a test and a characteristic movement in their excursion.

Grasping the Standards of Openness Treatment

•Continuous Methodology: Making sense of the idea of beginning with less scary parts of a trepidation and step by step stirring up to additional difficult experiences.

•Precise Desensitization: Prologue to matching unwinding procedures with openness to really diminish the apprehension reaction.

•Adjustment: Showing the rule that rehashed openness to a trepidation can lessen its force over the long haul.

Arranging Your Openness Technique

•Recognizing Openness Progressive systems: Direction on making a rundown of dreaded circumstances requested from least to most tension inciting, filling in as a guide for openness works out.

•Setting Clear, Reachable Objectives: Ways to characterize what achievement resembles at each phase of openness, guaranteeing objectives are explicit, quantifiable, and time-bound.

Executing Openness Procedures

•Independent Openness: How to securely and actually direct openness practices all alone, beginning with the least uneasiness instigating undertakings.

•Proficient Helped Openness: Talking about when and how to look for proficient assistance for directed openness treatment, especially for complex or profoundly imbued fears.

•Utilizing Augmented Reality (VR) and Reenactment: Investigating current advances that offer safe conditions for openness, particularly helpful for fears not effectively imitated, in actuality.

Practices for Successful Openness

•Openness Journal: Keeping an itemized diary of openness activities, sentiments, and progress, empowering self-reflection and change of techniques depending on the situation.

•Dread Confronting Difficulties: Organized exercises intended to direct perusers through their openness order, with methods for overseeing tension and commending triumphs.

•Unwinding and Establishing Methods: Supporting unwinding practices to use during openness works out, dealing with profound and actual responses.

Exploring Difficulties and Misfortunes

•Adapting to Expanded Uneasiness: Procedures for taking care of minutes when openness prompts elevated tension, underlining the significance of ingenuity and versatility.

•Changing the Openness Plan: How to alter your methodology in the event that specific openings are excessively difficult or not successful, guaranteeing a customized and adaptable procedure.

Past Openness: Keeping up with Progress

•Integrating Openness into Day to day existence: Ideas for coordinating openness practices into ordinary exercises, making dread a conflict a characteristic piece of life.

•Fostering a Drawn out Survival technique: Empowering perusers to see openness as a continuous device for overseeing fears, versatile to new feelings of dread that might arise from now on.

Embracing Openness as Strengthening

The section finishes up by reevaluating openness as a procedure for beating dread as well as a pathway to strengthening. It stresses how overcoming fears straightforwardly can prompt expanded self-assurance, flexibility, and opportunity. Perusers are reminded that openness is a course of development, requiring persistence and constancy, at the end of the day prompting a day to day existence less obliged by dread.

•Observing Achievements: Empowering perusers to perceive and praise each forward-moving step in their openness process, supporting the positive changes in their relationship with dread.

•Looking Forward: Planning perusers for the subsequent stages in their excursion, underscoring that openness is only one piece of a complete technique for overcoming fears.

Chapter 7: Step 6 – Acceptance and Adjustment

Prologue to Acknowledgment and Change

The part opens with an investigation of acknowledgment and change as fundamental parts of the trepidation overcoming process. It stresses that while openness straightforwardly stands up to dread, acknowledgment and change include embracing dread as a piece of the human experience and figuring out how to live with it in a solid and adjusted manner.

The Job of Acknowledgment in Defeating Dread

•Grasping Acknowledgment: Explaining that acknowledgment isn't about abdication or rout, yet about recognizing fears without allowing them to direct activities.

•The Force of Acknowledgment: Examining how tolerating dread can diminish its power and the hold it has over one's life, making it a less considerable rival.

The Course of Change

•Adjusting Methodologies: How to alter survival techniques as you develop and as your relationship with dread changes, guaranteeing they stay successful and significant.

•Life Past Trepidation: Imagining a daily existence where dread is overseen as opposed to destroyed, featuring the opportunity and flexibility that come from this mentality.

Systems for Developing Acknowledgment

•Care Works on: Consolidating care as an instrument for noticing fears without judgment, cultivating a more profound feeling of acknowledgment.

•Mental Adaptability: Fostering the capacity to change contemplations and points of view because of new data or changes in conditions.

•Self-Sympathy Activities: Strategies for rehearsing benevolence towards oneself in snapshots of dread, supporting the acknowledgment of one's weaknesses.

Acclimating to Another Typical

•Embracing Change: Empowering perusers to see changes in their relationship with dread as potential learning experiences, prompting a seriously satisfying life.

•Building a Steady Climate: Ways to establish an individual and social climate that upholds progressing development and transformation.

Practices for Acknowledgment and Change

•Acknowledgment Letter Composing: An activity that includes composing a letter to oneself, recognizing fears and communicating acknowledgment of them as a component of the excursion.

•The Adaptability Challenge: Exercises intended to rehearse mental adaptability, for example, intentionally changing schedules or attempting new ways to deal with critical thinking.

•Appreciation Journaling: Keeping a diary zeroed in on appreciation to move viewpoint from dread to enthusiasm for the excursion and development experienced.

Exploring Difficulties in Acknowledgment and Change

•Managing Backslide: Addressing how to oversee minutes when old feelings of dread reemerge, underlining the business as usual of this during the time spent acknowledgment and change.

•Keeping up with Inspiration: Techniques for remaining persuaded in the long haul, particularly when progress appears to be slow or when confronted with mishaps.

Acknowledgment and Change as Nonstop Development

The part finishes up by supporting that acknowledgment and change are not last objections but rather continuous cycles that add to a strong and versatile way to deal with life's difficulties, including dread. It motivates perusers to keep applying these standards, guaranteeing that the headway made in vanquishing fears is supported and based upon.

•Commending the Excursion: Empowering perusers to think about and praise the headway they've made, perceiving the strength they've created through confronting their feelings of trepidation.

•Forward Concentration: Looking forward to the future, this segment propels perusers to apply the standards of acknowledgment and acclimation to different everyday issues, advancing constant self-improvement and strengthening.

{ **8** }

Chapter 8: Step 7 - Mastery

Prologue to Dominance

The part opens by characterizing authority over dread as the capacity to perceive, comprehend, and oversee dread proactively. It stresses that authority is a continuous cycle, described by consistent learning and transformation. Dominance doesn't infer that dread does not exist anymore, but instead that an individual has what it takes and certainty to usefully explore dread.

Accomplishing Dominance Over Dread

•Attributes of Dominance: Portrays the characteristics of somebody who has dominated their apprehensions, including mindfulness, strength, adaptability, and mental fortitude.

•The Excursion from Dread to Dominance: A recap of the means taken to show up at authority, featuring how each step adds to a complete comprehension and the executives of dread.

Techniques for Keeping up with Dominance

•Ceaseless Picking up: Empowering an outlook of deep rooted finding out around oneself and the idea of dread, stressing that dominance is kept up with through continuous schooling and self-reflection.

•Versatile Ways of dealing with stress: Examining the significance of developing survival techniques to address new difficulties and fears as they emerge.

•Building a Dominance Outlook: Methods for cultivating a mentality that perspectives difficulties and fears as any open doors for development and learning.

Practices for Dominating Apprehension

•Dominance Planning: An activity to outline past triumphs in vanquishing fears, recognizing systems that worked and how they can be applied to future difficulties.

•The Test Rundown: Making a rundown of new difficulties or fears to handle, involving it as a method for applying dominance abilities and develop.

•Care and Reflection Customs: Laying out normal practices for care and reflection to remain associated with one's internal state and oversee fears proactively.

The Job of Local area in Authority

•Sharing Information and Encounters: Empowering perusers to impart their excursion and experiences to other people who are attempting to vanquish their feelings of dread, cultivating a feeling of local area and common help.

•Searching Out Coaches: The significance of finding and gaining from people who have accomplished dominance over their apprehensions, acquiring motivation and direction from their encounters.

Exploring Difficulties with Dominance

•Seeing Difficulties as Learning Amazing open doors: Reevaluating mishaps not as disappointments but rather as important encounters for learning and development.

•Flexibility Despite Backslide: Techniques for keeping up with strength and inspiration when old feelings of trepidation reemerge, utilizing the abilities created through the excursion to recapture control.

Determination: Embracing Dominance as a Lifestyle

The section closes by praising the peruser's excursion to authority, recognizing the difficult work, mental fortitude, and determination it required. It supports that dominance over dread is definitely not a static accomplishment yet a unique interaction that upgrades one's life and prosperity. Dominance is introduced as a lifestyle, a way to deal with living that embraces difficulties, invites development, and sees dread not as a foe but rather as an educator.

•The Steadily Developing Excursion: A forward-looking explanation that urges perusers to keep applying the standards of dominance to all everyday issues, seeing the victory of dread as only the start of a long lasting excursion of strengthening and self-revelation.

•A Source of inspiration: Persuading perusers to bring their dominance into the world, to show others how its done, and to help other people on their ways to vanquishing their feelings of dread, consequently making an expanding influence of strengthening.

Conclusion

Pondering the Excursion

The end starts by welcoming perusers to stop and ponder the excursion they have embraced. From the underlying acknowledgment and affirmation of their apprehensions to the engaging accomplishment of authority, each step has been urgent in changing their relationship with dread. This reflection underscores the mental fortitude, strength, and ingenuity expected to set out on such an excursion, recognizing the difficulties confronted and the development accomplished.

The Extraordinary Force of Overcoming Dread

Featuring the extraordinary effect of vanquishing dread, this part repeats how dominating trepidation prompts a really satisfying and enabled life. It examines the freshly discovered opportunity, certainty, and open doors that emerge when dread no longer directs one's decisions, praising the freedom from dread's limitations.

The Consistent Idea of Authority

While the aide finishes in the dominance of dread, this part highlights that dominance is definitely not a last objective yet a consistent cycle. It underlines the significance of continuous work on, learning, and variation in keeping up with dominance over dread, empowering perusers to see this as a long lasting excursion of development and self-disclosure.

Applying Authority Past Apprehension

Broadening the utilization of the standards realized, this part rouses perusers to apply their dominance over dread to different parts of their lives. It recommends that the abilities, mentalities, and bits of knowledge acquired can improve individual connections, vocation desires, and life's heap difficulties, offering instances of how dominance over dread converts into more extensive life authority.

A Call to Share and Move

In the soul of local area and backing that has been a string all through the aide, this last segment approaches perusers to impart their excursion and triumphs to other people. By becoming signals of mental fortitude and strength, they can motivate and uphold other people who are battling with dread, adding to a culture of strengthening and common development.

Shutting Words

The end closes with inspirational statements and strengthening, reaffirming the peruser's capacity to vanquish fears and overcome existence with mental fortitude and certainty. It reminds perusers that they are in good company on this excursion and that the fortitude to confront and vanquish dread is inside us all, ready to be released.

Goodbye and Forward

Offering one last goodbye, this part welcomes perusers to look forward with positive thinking, outfitted with the apparatuses and information to valiantly explore life's difficulties. It closes with a persuasive message, encouraging perusers to embrace the excursion ahead with an open heart and a daring soul, prepared to overcome any feelings of dread that emerge.

Appendices

Appendix A: Further Reading and Resources

This section offers a curated list of books, articles, websites, and videos that provide deeper insights into understanding and conquering fears. It includes:

- Self-Help Books: Titles that offer strategies and insights into overcoming various fears and anxieties.
- Scientific Articles: Accessible summaries of research findings on the psychology of fear and effective coping mechanisms.
- Websites and Online Forums: Recommended platforms where individuals can find communities and discussions focused on personal growth and fear management.
- Inspirational Videos: A selection of talks and documentaries that inspire courage and provide real-life success stories of overcoming fear.

Appendix B: Exercises and Worksheets

A collection of practical exercises and worksheets designed to apply the concepts discussed in the book. This includes:

- Fear Mapping Worksheet: A template to help readers map out their fears, triggers, and coping strategies.
- Goal-Setting Worksheet: A guide for setting SMART (Specific, Measurable, Achievable, Relevant, Time-bound) goals related to overcoming fears.

- Journal Prompts: A series of prompts to encourage reflective journaling about personal experiences with fear, progress made, and insights gained.
- Relaxation Techniques Guide: Step-by-step instructions for relaxation practices such as deep breathing, progressive muscle relaxation, and mindfulness meditation.

Appendix C: Professional Help and Support

This section provides information on when and how to seek professional help, including:

- Signs That Professional Help Is Needed: Identifying when fears or anxieties become overwhelming and interfere with daily life, signaling the need for professional intervention.
- Finding a Therapist: Tips for finding a qualified therapist or counselor, including resources and directories.
- Support Groups: Information on finding support groups for individuals facing similar fears or challenges.

Appendix D: Inspirational Quotes

A collection of motivational and insightful quotes about facing and overcoming fears. These quotes serve as quick sources of inspiration and encouragement for readers to reflect on and draw strength from.

Appendix E: FAQs on Conquering Fears

Answers to frequently asked questions about conquering fears, addressing common concerns, misconceptions, and practical advice for individuals at different stages of their journey.

Appendix F: Acknowledgments

An acknowledgment section thanking everyone who contributed to the creation of the book, including experts consulted, individuals who shared their stories, and anyone else who played a role in bringing the guide to life.